NO EARTHLY REASON?

Thank you!

All the Best
with your Work
Liz R

crocus

c r o c u s

NO EARTHLY REASON?

Poetry On Green Issues

First published in 1989 by Crocus

Crocus books are published by
Commonword Ltd,
Cheetwood House,
21 Newton Street,
Manchester M1 1FZ.

Commonword gratefully acknowledges financial assistance from the Association of Greater Manchester Authorities, North West Arts Association and Manchester City Council.

Typeset and printed by Rap Ltd, Rochdale, OL12 7AF.

British Library Cataloguing in Publication Data
No earthly reason?: poetry on green issues.
1. Poetry in English, 1945- — Anthologies
821'.914'08

ISBN 0 946745 65 X

CONTENTS

Foreword

Long, long, ago, in the days before I became a 'scientist', I edited a poetry magazine called 'Great Works', whose title was intended to undermine and satirise all such titles. I studied modern literature and had a wonderful time, as you can imagine. I was an anarchist, an apathist, and, of course, a hedonist. I loved the city, as one does. Credentials are, by definition, necessary, if one is to be believed.

But before that I was a young boy growing up amongst cows and hens and tractors. All my spare time was taken up by an overwhelming interest in the natural world, particularly in entomology. There seemed no distinction between the cows and the butterflies, nor between the crop of kale and the weeds left by the rabbits around the field perimeter. All were part of an integrated, self regulating system, in which we played a part. Returning to these innate values with less innocence and less certainty, brings a fierce determination to protect what is the cornerstone of my own existence, as it is more fundamentally of everyone's.

What has all this to do with these poems? Not a lot perhaps. I do know however that the writers are expressing ideas, sometimes contradictory, but in themselves truthful, with which I strongly empathise. The problems we, in our common environment, face, are highly complex, and need expression. We all change, whether our surroundings change or not, as internal and external forces alter our perspectives. The late Sir Peter Scott, father figure of the green movement, started his adult life as a hunter of the very birds he later came to protect so effectively. This is not a contradiction.

Unfortunately the luxury of choice in such matters is rapidly being taken away from us. Our capacity to see beauty and to wonder will not go away, whatever happens — as one writer says, oil on water can be most attractive. I think there is an unclear distinction between what we like and what we value. We like the comforts and security of a rich Western World, we like travel, and luxury, and children. All these may destroy the World.

I, like many of these writers, love the natural world for

itself. Yes, we can do small important things, like saving energy, recycling where possible, reducing our personal contribution to pollution, finding organic methods of feeding the teeming millions, and writing. These poems help to show us where we have been, where we are, and where we don't want to go.

Bill Symondson
Presenter, BBC's *Gardener's World*

Introduction

No Earthly Reason? is a green book in the sense that it examines issues that affect our environment and our daily lives. The poems in this collection move from global issues such as deforestation and third world debt, to the food we eat and the dramatic changes occuring in our cities and streets. Whilst the writers in *No Earthly Reason?* are united in their concern for the environment, there is a great diversity in their approach to the issue.

Some people may regard all environmental issues as dull but worthy, but there is a good deal of humour to be found amongst these pages. Diane R. Pickering's 'Five Mile Hike' is a wry portrait of 'man' ill at ease with the great outdoors, while Mark Abraham's 'The Rime of the Savage Goldfish' is gentle whimsy at its serious best! Pat Amick's 'Trouble in North Dakota' explores farming and the profit motive with a fierce irony, and 'Burger Beast' by Maria Maryon forecasts a number of unfortunate consequences for the west's over-indulgence in its favourite food. P. D. Cookson's 'I've Gone Green' is an unrestrained and hilarious rant against political hypocrisy.

But there is of course a more serious side to all this. In 'A Human Perpective' Cath Staincliffe communicates a sense of wonder and awe, as well as sadness, at the spoilt potential of the Earth, and our difficult relationship with the planet. She pursues this theme further in 'Nuclear Fear', by depicting a mother's apprehension at a militarised present and the possibility of a similar future. Lorna Euphemia Griffiths' 'I Remember' poignantly recounts her regret at the erasure from the landscape of childhood haunts, while 'Ozone Children' offers a futuristic nightmare, and reminds us of the stark choices which face us today. In 'Zebra Shoes' Steve Rouse roundly condemns the abuses of the fur trade, whilst the desire for freedom and change is given voice in Georgina A. Blake's 'The dolphin's home is not a pool in a zoo . . .'. The changes taking place in towns, cities and whole regions are examined in the savage irony of 'North England Theme Park', and the anger of Julie Armstrong-Colton's 'Rainbows Lost'.

Yet underpinning *No Earthly Reason?* is the will to celebrate the world around us, and the desire to communicate a message of hope for the future. Peggy Stockwell's 'Continuity' portrays nature's ability to renew itself, whilst 'Broth' by Steven Waling explores new possibilities within the old idea of 'living within your means'. In 'Chipko Andolan' one route of resistance to deforestation is joyfully explained, and Di Williams' 'Song For The Freshwater Mussel' is a hymn for the preservation of a little known bivalve. 'Autumn Crocus' by Elaine Tebay, celebrates survival against the odds, and 'Focused' proposes an agenda where words, like wayside flowers, alter and shape the world in most unexpected senses.

These are just a small selection from *No Earthly Reason?* These poems open up new ways of looking at — and changing — the world we live in. We would like to thank the members of the editorial group who made the final selection for the book, from the hundreds of poems that were submitted by writers across the North West. They were: Michael Nolan — the Monday Night Group, Anne Robinson — Commonword's Publications Committee, and Pete Wilson — Manchester Friends of the Earth. Their support, commitment and enthusiasm, were invaluable.

Helen Windrath
Commonword

In Swaledale

A special contribution to *No Earthly Reason?*
by Mike Harding

In Swaledale lal Tommy Woof sits up,
A lone cow calving in the byre's his charge.
She nuzzles the stall and Tommy fills his cup
From the flask. Above the Corpse Way and the yard

A hard moon rubs the margin of the dale,
Troubled by coming clouds.
A yowe stands, graven by the river's edge
A bat, a sudden slash in the air sails out

Orbits the barn once and is gone. From a ledge
As a light rain starts to fall, hunting owls call.

In Dentdale lovers lie below a bridge
Entangled legs and soft cries and soft calls,
A tawny owl slides overhead sweet as a moth
Sees the pale flesh hears the murmurs fall.

In Ribblesdale a signal-man talks down
The line to Settle, horse names, odds, times,
And the television news, family, friends;
Celebrating the ways of men to men.

And over all of this, Lal Tommy's house,
The signal box, the lovers in the barn
Softer than the dust from any moth's wing,
Softer than the skin of any calf.

Softer than any lover's wet-mouthed after-kiss
The soft rain from Chernobyl falls.

We aren't the whole of this world, or even the sum of its parts. We are a small span in a complex web of things living and dead and everything, from the eagle to the earthworm is as vital to this web and has as much right to play its part in the whole story as man. Unless we realise this we are doomed.

A Tree

Cath Staincliffe

A tree
To mark the spot.
To shelter, shade.
To sacrifice the old king
And crown the new.
To house the goddess.

A tree
To lie under kissing
To run around laughing
To climb up, to cling to,
To build a house in.
To swing from.
To tell the seasons.
To count the time.

A tree
To last beyond me.

Elm Pennies

Di Williams

Elm pennies on the ground,
Easy currency,
Scattered the wind knows where,
Of no account.
But one year there may be no
Elm pennies,
No elm trees.
Heed what the wind may bring,
What hidden spores,
And count nothing as neglectable,
As safe in the bank,
Not even trees.

Gasping

Pat Amick

We may reap a bigger harvest
weave a cheaper cloth — untouched
by hand or benediction — but

the circle has been broken.

When the misfit left outside
to sniff the wind protests in vain
the gods are leaving

an eternity has lost its meaning.

They linger on the edges —
gasping over temples dwarfed as counting houses
scrape the heavens where

the ozone has a hole in it.

Industrial Heritage

Cath Staincliffe

It used to be filthy,
Dark satanic mills,
Trolley buses broken down
In yellow fog,
Gritty, sulphuric taste in the mouth.

Not now.
They've sandblasted it all.
Clean Air Act.
No smoke now,
Spick and span.
Tourist trade, Industrial Heritage,
They've even brought the trolley buses back.

The new pollution's invisible, see.
Doesn't dirty the buildings.
Radiation and that,
Lead, acid rain, you know.
Fantastic.
Looking at the place,
No sign,
You'd never know.
Can't even see the hole in the sky from here.
And that global warming's
Improving the climate for visitors.

I've heard it said,
That the virulent sunsets we get
Are due more to the muck in the atmosphere
Than to the beauty in nature.
Troublemakers, Worrymongers.
Some people are never satisfied.
Well...
What the eye doesn't see,
The heart can't grieve over.

Farming Today

Jean Tarry

Little boy blue, come blow up your program.
The rape now yields coconut, sheep produce ham.
Where is the man who is playing with genes?
He's in the laboratory, making square beans.
Will you enlighten him? No, not I
For he's making E.C. mountains in the sky.

Hearing Things

Marguerite Gazeley

As I sit here
chomping hungrily
upon a round
of beef inside a bun
I hear a strange unsettling...
Thud!...it goes
Thud! Thud!...

It's like the sound
of cattle hooves
upon the ground
or echoes
of axes on a tree
so far away...
further than the eye can see.

Why am I hearing things?
What has all this to do with me?

Burger Beast

Maria Maryon

The giant thing,
With the hamburger head,
Ate everything in its sight.
But for its favourite food,
It had to bend,
Way down,
To the ground,
To catch small children.
'Scrunch, Scrunch',
How it loved to crunch them.

It was a nightmarish day.
As it came to life,
People finally realised,
They were not eating food,
At all,
The food was eating them.

The hamburger thing,
Created by men,
Was fooled by women.
They shouted up at it,
It slowly nodded its head.

This was the deal.
'Since Frankensteins, in the end,
Always turn on their makers',
They said,
'Save yourself some trouble,
Why not eat the men, instead.'

Everyone agreed how peaceful it was,
Once the last man,
Disappeared down the thing's bun.

The Reintroduction of Extinct Species Into Britain

Jean Tarry

Did you know that
Hippopotamuses are indigenous to Yorkshire?
They frolicked fatly,
Fruitfully twenty thousand years ago, in the Dales.

It follows that
Hippopotamuses are very like Geoffrey Boycott:
Yorkshire through and through.
Let's ask for some to be sent back home from Africa.

Natural History

Michael Hall

There are glass showcases, huge antique displays
Of stuffed and muted birds. They frighten us first year
boys
Whose thoughts are still of mothers and of toys.

I smell the stink of death from the things behind the
glass
Their faded brilliances caught forever in a dinge of
feathered tat,
And harsh bead eyes that stare and pierce my back.

Stiff frozen poses give no hint of what must have been
Nothing now except a dull and faded sheen
Which tells us that history, not nature, here is framed
And freedom captured cannot be contained.

Zebra Shoes

Steve Rouse

Dressed to kill,
with
imitation eyes,
imitation ears,
imitation noses,
and
real skin,
the shoes stand on their shelf
and patiently await
the arrival of
a customer
without inconvenient
principles
or taste.

When I put
my new shoes on,
I found they were
already warm;

And though the weather
was fine,
they felt wet inside -
as if something
oozed
between my toes.

As the night wore on
my new shoes became
increasingly
uncomfortable
for dancing.
They seemed to stiffen
and began to pinch

my feet
quite painfully.

When I took them off
I found my feet were
bleeding,
though I could find
no trace
of any injury.

Put on your zebra shoes
and dance the night away.

Feel the body's warmth,
the quickened pulse,
the shallow breath,
the crack of bones,
the crunch of gristle,
the skinner's knife,
the rictus of death.

Feel the blood flow around
your pretty painted toes.

Put on your zebra shoes
and dance the night away!

Ladybird Ladybird

Gill Blease

Bead of blood red
Boasting polka dot black.
Enamelled red ladies,
Light up your feet,
Fly away home.
Your house is flickering.
Your children are stifling.
And we are exposed, like thieves,
Red Handed.

Parasite Man Haiku

Jean Tarry

The Tree of Life fed
knowledge, not wisdom, becomes
poisoning ivy.

Ideas

Pete Wilson

Ideas required, flooding through mind
edited as they go
into oblivion.

Recall from oblivion is not possible, that oblivion that
cannot be real;
rather refer to it as limbo, a vague deep grey area
beyond direct recall,
volumes of space beyond specific definition
whose indefinite edges feel
too close to oblivion.

Ideas required, like the calling of the hard sell
where they can be imprisoned in print,
beat up by brain police, left
twisted and limp
and a verdict of accidental death passing all
understanding
can be brought
from a local book cellar.

Ideas that require sorting,
policing into coherence,
obedience.

Rare vintages can be found, and lost,
burnt with rainforest precision for the celebration,
the flesh of our spirit turning, burning,
turning on the global spit of convulsive consumption.

Slick oily film of phlegm buoyant, floating,
pictured on dying oceans where whales cry
one to another
across barely fathomable depths, cataloguing
yet another great rape case.

Is the plea to be ignorance or insanity?

A glasshopper's thoughts flit like whining chains,
soaring
through living biomass, in communion
with a world bank bottle planting scheme.
Ignorance and insanity, we are all guilty.

The ancient sailor's salty tears will avenge
the tortured beast in eustatic glory
as the flesh of the earth roasts in the light of its only
sun
and clashing symbols ring in the new,
and out with the old.

Only the sharing of ideas can be outlawed.

Focused

Peggy Stockwell

Among the chippings
By the railway line
Stood the row of lupins,
Purple blues and pinks,
Only noticed when
The train had slowed.

There they were straight
And stiff as they glowed,
        jerking my mind
From its wanderings to
The present — hot June day,
A dusty stifling carriage.

More lupins, lilac,
Rhododendrons in bloom
        along the way.
Seeds blown on the wind,
Escaped from gardens
Unrestricted by fences
And the weeding hand
Had found anchorage

On wasteland — unforced,
Left to grow in peace, space
To spread and flourish —
They nourish the eyes
Of passers-by in
Their brief blossoming...

Can WORDS do the same?
Can they find their niche
Borne on the breeze
From an open mind?

A Human Perspective

Cath Staincliffe

From space
The coast of Madagascar
Frills sweet lace
Across the cobalt
Of an ocean's sway.
Daybreak over arced horizons
Light rims the curve
Rays split across the globe.
The world turns.

From space
The thin blue shell of atmosphere
Washes rose
Sudden sunrise
Bursts across the backbone of the Andes
Pours into lagoons
Paints atolls in coral
Warms the earth.
The world turns.

From space
Storms flash across
The Malaspina glacier
Dance down to Manitoba
Skate over the ice
Leap above forests
Traverse waters bright then deep
Tumble around the vast Pacific.
The world turns.

From space
Behold
The veined continent of Africa
Gold, green and brown.
Volcano, savannah,

The red-ribbed dunes of the Namib desert
Rocked on the cradle
Of steady blue waters.
The world turns.

The cosmonauts, the astronauts,
Have seen it all,
And weep.

Broth

Steven Waling

I

The high fells, clear
as the first thought:
and the sun leaping
over my table like a hare.

I was thinking
as the train
sent me through
why stay in one place
for longer than it takes
to grow this skin
of impressions,

like an onion peeled
and cut into squares
for broth?

II

        A broth
I drink each day
on the train

tastes of rivers
hills the thick stock
of survival:
                vegetables
dropped in the pan

that's kept filled up
with swede carrots
potato:

whatever
happens to be around

is a meal to be made of.

Five Mile Hike

Diane R. Pickering

Bob feels dressed for
the job. Four old women
used to the outdoors.
Twittering, Bob knows —
a symphony of abuse.
Bob feels sweat all over

shoes too tight
he passes a hand
over his head.
His ear-ring glints
an old woman pounces
like a magpie.
Bob smiles, 'Hot day?'

The old women vaguely
grasp the sky,
like a curtain
pulling it over the day.
Bob inhales slowly on a
cigarette, snorting like a horse.
A cow chews its cud.

Fell Walking

Cath Staincliffe

Up in the dales
Where the air cuts clean,
Three valleys lay below
Draped in silver-green baize
Dotted with the trails
Of dry-stone walling
Specked with sheep
Scored by springs and streams.
Age-old stone built settlements
Rooted in the dips
Where the rivers meet.
I walk along a bridleway
A thousand years old.
Time to let my thoughts drift,
Peace, recreation...
SHATTERED by the roar of a jet fighter
Who spends the afternoon
On imaginary bombing missions
Blasting us all to hell.

Waste ground — by the A580

Di Williams

They are put coal lumps in the roots of the tree
On bended broken branches, sharp-springing stubbble
And the roots is made flat, squashed
And the whole of the growth spreaded outwards and
then up.
Coal and other rubbish in the den of the tree heart
And old iron under the branches and on the grass,
Cans and bedspring and the binding from packing
cases sharp,
And we found one shoe, good new one and an old
worn one with it
Lying dry under the grass and the bending branches
Where the lorries hurtle by all the time but nobody
goes.

Faith Street

Pat Amick

No holocaust has happened here,
no catastrophic bombs
have fallen — dereliction
came about inaudibly
— the closing of the factories
excited little movement
once the apparatus of the State
had shown it knows a thousand ways
of dealing with dissent.

A giant B & Q is open Sundays here
in place of Chapel
— crowded car parks where
the Sunday School once stood
and taught us all disdain for Mammon.

Who can leave these crumbling terraces?
Conversion of the narrow road
to by-pass means the Pelican
may light our way to sudden
and conclusive crossing over!

Calm and skilful neighbours
will not sorrowfully dress our bodies
— go collecting door to door
to grace us with a worthy wreath
— or stand about in silent witness
as we make our final exit.

Enterprising lads will come
to make a packet
from the clearance of our houses
— grab them cheap for speedy renovation.

Subtle weapons have been activated here

— releasing slow, insidious poison,
culminating in the smooth
obliteration of our world
without the firing of a single shot.

The Blue Route

Elaine Tebay

They came in crowds
houses
gnawing the land.

The houses needed people,
2.5 children
and a car.

Soon, shops school roads,
a power station
gorged their fill.

Green belt status
manipulated,
capitulated.

Objections?
Overruled.

Three farms remain,
hugging a river
and park.

The people
from the houses
value the land.

They need the open space
for their children
and dog.

Soon a land hungry
motorway will
satisfy its appetite.

Green belt status
manipulated,
capitulated.

Objections?
Overruled.

North England Theme Park

Jane McNulty

I live in the North England Theme Park
To the west of Enterprise City
It's based on 'Industrial History'
It isn't meant to be pretty
My mates are all on a Job-scheme
That pays ten quid plus the Dole
They're there to entertain tourists
By digging and refilling holes
And me, I work as a waitress
At the new 'King Cotton Cafe'
Only the Government call it 'training'
So I don't get my fair day's pay
It's not that we're always complaining
We've still got a roof for our heads
But when they finally sell-off the Council
They'll charge rent for a park bench instead
There are some that get drunk and fall over
Thre are some that just cry in the street
The Police round them up every morning —
That way the pavements stay neat
There's something all wrong in the Theme Park
The Yuppies come up for a laugh
And ask if we've heard the War's over
Ask if we keep coal in the bath
Well for them the war may be over
To them this decade's been kind
But us who live in this Dream Park
Those ten years have left us behind.

Shades of Green

Pat Amick

An eyesore — just a useless piece of land
before this new development was planned.

Some locals came for so-called recreation
— wasted on the younger generation.

Now supervised activities all day
attract a nicer class prepared to pay

for them. Our garage will promote Lead Free,
the supermarket stocks no C.F.C.

All food containers are degradable,
we place No Smoking signs on every table.

Values here are represented in
well tended borders of abundant green.

Call The Tune

K. M. McDonnell

It's the pound in your pocket they're after,
So that's what you use to get through.
Just read through this verse 'fore you open your purse
And they'll listen to your point of view.
They'll turn green if it shows them a profit.
They'll tailor their wares to your taste.
So make your selection from 'Ozone protection'
To 'Bio-degradable waste'.
If Brazil's where they ship out your corned-beef,
Then don't buy it the next time you shop.
It's your protestation 'gainst deforestation
And you'll buy it again when they stop.
Don't buy Nissans or Nikons or Sanyos
'Cause the Whalers set out from Japan
When they see it's the whaling they'll stop the fleet
  sailing,
They're entrepreneurs to a man!
If the greenhouse effect is unnerving,
Lower power consumption's your choice.
More reticient use of electrical juice
Gives your feelings a powerful voice.
So when shopping for things in the market,
Consider the Earth's present state.
Avoid buys that spell danger for our planetary manger
It's you that determines our fate.
So for whatever issues disturb you
Let the culprits endure a cash loss.
Where your cash is concerned let them change 'til it's
  earned.
It's your cash, it's your world, you're the boss.

Food For Thought

Cath Staincliffe

Steroids in beef
Salmonella in eggs
Dioxin in nappies
Nitrates in veg.
Toxins in water
Hormones in milk
God's in his heaven
The world's feeling ill.

Earth Matters

Gwyneth Cleworth

Do you still want,
All your Jacks and Jills,
To wander and play,
On lush green hills?

Do you want them to drink,
The waters, so clear,
And fill up their lungs,
For many a year.

With clean fresh air,
Their right — from birth?
Then please protect,
Our gift of earth.

Its yield is unfailing,
We reap with joy,
Whilst man can build,
So can man destroy.

Our air is polluted,
And rivers and seas,
Feed death and destruction,
To livestock and trees.

Chemicals forge the link,
In every known guise,
From the depths of the oceans,
To the acid rain skies.

Let's not leave a legacy,
Of barren decay,
Earth matters for our children's
Tomorrows today!

Autumn Crocus

Elaine Tebay

When I first saw you
I was astonished by your presence,
by your fragile beauty,
your luminous lavender hue.
I had not known of your existence
until that Autumn day
when we met by chance.
From that moment
thirty years ago
we've been friends.

Each yearly pilgrimage
confirms your survival,
rekindles my existence.
You've been myself
striving fruition
my Phoenix, my confidante,
on occasions you've been my sanity,
Always you've been
my salve
before the dread of winter.

Soon you are to be removed,
for your own safety, your survival,
for a number on a map.
Until now the threat has
been man's ignorance,
but this, this is an Army
of bureaucracy, of politics
in whose midst you and I
are of no consequence,
sacrificed for the M66.

Continuity

Peggy Stockwell

Trees in every garb,
Bare, bereft of leaves,
Decked in fresh spring green;
Full, fat in Summer,
Flushed with Autumn's gold
        glorious array,
Before the Fall's drift
Does settle down. Thrifty
Nature renews itself —
Rich mulch feeds fresh seeds.

Lament For A Tree

To the editors of the church magazine who were putting blank sheets at the end of each copy.

Margaret Rich

More years ago than I can count
God our Father gave me life
And caused me to stand upright
Beneath His blessed sun.
As He commanded I gave shelter and shade;
Food for birds and small animals.
My pleasure was in knowing
That I did His will.
The passing years took my brothers away,
Always with hope in their hearts:
A chair, a desk, a table,
An altar;
A cross.

Now it is my turn:
The time for which I have waited.
And did I wait
For this?

Chipko Andolan

Cath Staincliffe

She hugs the tree
Skin against bark
No wind stirs its canopy
The tree is listening.
In the distance
The whine of machinery
The drone of a generator.

She hugs the tree
Her form a bright dab
Of colour at the bottom
Of the old-old trunk.
The patterns of the bark
Echoed in the network of lines
Around her knuckles
Across her strong hands.

She knows
This tree has to be saved
She understands
The balance.
The way life supports life
And death breeds death.
She sees —
The trees bind the earth
The trees hold up the sky.

She and her sisters
A hundred strong
Hug the trees
Till chainsaws fall silent
A muttered retreat,
Peals of laughter
Ring through the glades.

We have won.
We hugged the trees.
We saved the forest.

After writing this poem, based on hearsay, I found out the facts: in 1973 in Gopeshwar, India, local villagers hugged trees and saved them from destruction. The movement, called Chipko Andolan, spread round the world.

Excuses

Debjani Chatterjee

In London world leaders meet in Economic Summit
to thrash out, over champagne, the problem of third
world debt.

Who cannot hear Somalia calling? And Biafra,
Ethiopia, Sudan? ... Like tidal waves they plummet.
Is there room in politics for empathy with despair?
Earthquake, famine, flood, disease; homeless, starving
refugees,
silenced and maimed by selfish hate, victims of
landgrabbing,
ideological tyrannies and the different
hungers of the powerful. They suffer because humans
alienate and reject their kind. I would forget them too
but their misery follows me home from the market place;
they leap from newsprint and t.v., and when there is silence
I suspect press censorship, government embarrassment.
Even with senses closed against them, the spirit thrashes
outraged at successive waves of pain. Their situation
places me in mine and I have no respite. They devour
me in raw, raw places.

Strange how one notices people's sexuality, race,
colour, language, religion, nationality and tribe...
'How many inches is your nose? What backstreet made
your 'R's
slur just so?' Fears and prejudices build a great divide.
We reassure ourselves by sporting conformist o.k.
badges on cannon-fodder chests that tell us we are not
them. Inside, an essential humanity escapes us.

Yes, Tibetan lama in tattered robes, violence stained,
I have a bowl of tearful soup I would gladly give you
with no thought of karma. Will it sustain your war-torn
land?

Oppressed black brother, will my lone cheer feed your famished dreams?
My shoulders are not broad enough though my arms are wide when
you lean on me, Bangladesh. I have only neighbourly
talk to erase the rape and slaughter. But your memory
burns bitter in my brain. Words are few and poor for the mind
explodes — fragments. I have the comfort of perpetual shock.

Cambodian mother, which of your children would you feed
with my rice bowl and three beansprouts? How many mouths and meals?
And how many empty?
My conscience won't swallow the reproach of ignored stomachs;
I did not cause this. I will not choose among the dying,
who to succour. I am not God. He has much to answer.
So I withhold the soup, rice, beansprouts. I withdraw myself
and overeat, ulcerous with worry, and die early,
quietly, each time I watch the belly of starvation,
or a child's dreadful stare.

Gandhi wiped a single tear, Mother Theresa cuddled
an orphan. All count to make the sound of one hand clapping.
Where is the lean Spaniard now and where his faithful friend?
It's better to tilt at windmills, a basin on the head.

Without the third world there would be no first, but who will put
the whole world first? Greed is bottomless. Those who will not share
wealth, safeguard it by pretence at Economic Summit.

I am impoverished of excuses, but bear with me;
today my grandchild's teddybear's stuffing has fallen out.

Trouble in North Dakota

(or Is This What They Mean By 'Enemies Within', Ma?)

Pat Amick

Please God don't let it rain!
The holders of commodities had counted on the
failure of the crops in North Dakota — where
the passing band of cloud creates
a panic in the trading pits — and prices falling
faster than the board can register produce an
agitated mass of upright sellers' hands.

...The farmers watch
the sky with quiet desperation
— after winds and frost
and baneful heat — they still sustain a fierce
though very distant hope.

...Good news — the threat of rain is over,
wheat is up — by 50 cents a bushel,
traders are again in buoyant mood;
— in 1988 you guys
we're heading for the biggest profit-making
drought we've ever seen!

Waiting For Water

Joan Poulson

I wait here
every day
every day
I wait
for water

the inside
of my mouth
is dry
as dry as
the earth
which rises
to each movement
of my feet

when the well
is open
I will fill
the pot
fill it
to the brim
with water

I will dip
my lips
into the wetness

I will let
my tongue
lap
at the cool
wetness

and press
my face

into the shining
surface
of the water

I will feel
the wetness
through my body

and will hold
that feeling
as each
wet drop
rolls
from my face
to drip
back
safe
among the rest

and my mouth
will sing
the wetness

as I carry
home
my jar

brimming
still
with water.

Ozone Children

Lorna Euphemia Griffiths

She stands on scorching dirt
aside withered vegetation
Her naked skin stripped purple
and blistered
Dogs fight children for water
Babies suckle powdered milk
She doesn't move —
She has no choice but to turn
a blind eye.

Seasons

Jerry Middleton

Seasons 'Yeah I remember them'
They used to bring life
Regularly on a quarterly basis

Then one day
Man stopped paying the bills
And we were
Cut off

Green

Julia Damassa

Outside the supermarket
sign the petition
'SAVE OUR EARTH'.

Feel a momentary
sense of achievement
as you turn the ignition.

Rainbows Lost

Julie Armstrong-Colton

Once green now...
Tired sad streets licked with grime,
where pavements sweat rainbows
and alleys breath stinks sour as fine drizzle
climbs onto the backs of
unfed cats alone.

Once flowers now...
Gutters glitzy with crushed fag ends, papers
and chasers
as razored children play,
day bleeds away.
Knots silently gather,
dirty grey eyes in dirty grey faces,
faint floating faces, shunt places, alone.

Once tranquility now...
Scabbed buildings blistered.
Fat fire hangs thick as
time
to spew out
echoes do shout!
Wait for the clout, clout, clout.

Fast flying feet.

Once life now...
The wail of a siren.
The scream of a train.
Puddles of life trickle down a drain.

Majestic Grand

Georgina A. Blake

progress
gapes
where once it stood

Majestic Grand

swing doors leading
from

genteel
graffiti-free

photographic
past

to
parks
for
cars.

Shadows and Panes

Peggy Stockwell

In the vast bed
In the narrow room
Safe from a world of gloom
I bury myself
In fantasy —
Snuggled between
Musty-smelling sheets —
Peering at lines lit
By a lone candle,
Forgetting for a while
The grim streets.

Word pictures are brighter
Than the drab-grey-day
Reality that I shirk.
Shadows flicker on
The dun walls thrown
By unsteady gaslight
In the next room
Welcoming my
Mother home from work.

Outside, cowls atop
Chimney pots whirl and dance
In tune to the wind's advance.
That wind roars and whines
Through ill-fitting sashes,
Rattling window-frames
Splashing rain on panes —
A symphony that
Accompanies restless dreams,
Above, the roof holds
Half the sky at bay.

Come the day, through

The mean window I see —
Blackened brick, topped
By wet grey slate
Capped by a strip
Of scudding cloud — I feel
As flat as that
Colourless plate
Of glass, dreading the trip
To the outside tap...
To fill the pail to
Wash the sleep away.

Cold-water-clean
In the classroom,
Mesmerized by
The scene as I gaze on
Slate grey rain on grey slate
Above soot smudged brick
And peeling paint.
The wind still howls
And cowls strain upon
Their chimney pots
Trailing veils of grey.

I, hear her droning voice dull
Until it turns shrill,
Feel sick in the pit
Of my stomach —
Window-gazing is
Forbidden by teacher
Who promises prizes
And treats that are
Self-righteously withdrawn.

The memories are still
As clear as those high
Rain-washed windows were —
And are no more.

I Remember

Lorna Euphemia Griffiths

Armed with cardboard boxes we run
to get our place on the bank-come-slide.
Free laughter splinters the air
Screams echo their delight
as we rough and tumble
through the beckoning grass.
Dirty dresses and torn jeans
are the least of our worries
as pleasure is our aim.
To skim stones across the water's surface,
to fish for frogs and newts,
to play hide and seek or kiss catch
between the trees with bold leaves and branches
that umbrella the picnic hampers.
I remember where I played as a child.
I cannot bring my child there now
for rows of dark, hard flats and houses
and long grey lines of motorway
replace my fond memories
of boisterous laughter
and soft green.

Beautiful Dereliction

Tim Court

Reclamation, gentrification,
We can't have wilderness.
Nature's hand is forced,
Her bones are crushed
Under concrete.
This is beautiful,
This dereliction.
The tall grasses wave
Their proud heads
In frantic appeal.
I hear them calling, they say
The orchids will die.

Fairies' Washing

Pat Amick

The pleasure gained from
things not understood.
Those uninstructed rambles,
childhood names — of
Scabbyhead and Knitbone,
One-o'clock and Piss-a-bed.
The treetops used to point
and whistle 'this way'
to the acquiescent wind,
who nudged me firmly on
while clouds would
overtake us for the fun of it.

A random fall of sticks
conveys a secret message
and a rainbow slick of oil
on water came from fairies
spreading out their washing.

The Rime of the Savage Goldfish

Mark Abraham

Beware the savage goldfish
With teeth like nine-inch nails!
A mighty chain-saw down his back
And razor-blades for scales!

Beware the savage goldfish!
Beware his evil eye!
For ever and ever and a day
He silently glides by!

He's twice as tall as Blackpool Tower,
And broad as the Isle of Man!
There is no fish or serpent yet
Can measure to his span.

The killer whales, the swordfish,
The sharks and the octopee!
They panic in their thousands
When the goldfish goes to sea!

For there is no stretch of water
No lake or river-bed
Where the awful savage goldfish
Has not raised his head.

There is no sea or ocean
From the equator to the poles
From which the savage goldfish
Has not gathered souls.

One day the savage goldfish
Was basking in the sun
With a tummy full of tugboats
After the day was done!

As the evening orb dipped in the sea
And darkness filled the sky
Something strange and eerie
Caught his evil goldfish eye.

For everywhere upon those waves
As the ocean turned to night
There danced a hundred thousand points
Of incandescent light.

The awful savage goldfish,
The terror of every shore,
Had never seen the like of this
In all his life before.

The water rose and the water fell,
His body dipped and turned,
But his skin, to what was luminous,
Tingled, twitched — and burned!

And now the savage goldfish
Was as meek as any lamb
As a hundred thousand points of fire
Pricked him as he swam!

The awful savage goldfish
Ran now before the tide.
He searched for bays and estuaries
Where he might safely hide.

But every wave that now he rode
Did glow as bright as day
And every slap of water seemed
To brand him as he lay.

Sparks flew from his nine-inch teeth
His scales grew hot as coals!
It seemed his mighty skin of steel
Was full of mighty holes.

And so the savage goldfish
Swam as fast as he could flee.
He did not know that humankind
Called this the Irish Sea!

He did not know or notice
A pipe from off the shore
Or how the glory all around
Came from the filth it bore.

And so he swam as fast he could
There was no time to wait,
Until he came to what humankind
Calls St George's Strait.

This was the open sea at last,
The broad Atlantic swell!
He swam and swam as every ship
Rang out its warning bell.

'Beware the savage goldfish!
Beware the teeth that bite!
Turn back your ships if you would live
To see the morning light!'

But the awful savage goldfish
Had one thing on his mind,
To swim as fast as ever he could
And leave the fires behind.

And now, he ran for pure relief
In the wide Atlantic space,
An empty coca-cola can
Smacked him in the face!

There came one more, and yet again
And then a bottle or two!
Until wherever he looked, such stuff
Completely filled his view.

The awful savage goldfish
Sank as deep as ever he could
And there he breathed the sea again
And knew that it was good!

But what was this, this brackish taste
That struck him as he swam?
That made him shut his goldfish mouth
As tight as any clam?

That made him squint his evil eye
That made him twist and stretch?
A taste that grew more brackish still
Till he began to retch?

Down there at the foot of the ocean
The goldfish was alone.
Of all the creatures of the sea
He was the only one.

The sharks and the octopusses,
The swordfish and the whales
Were now but pictures in a book,
No more than fairy tales!

The goldfish lost his nine-inch teeth
Dissolved in the acid sea!
His scales all blunt, his chain-saw back
As rusty as could be!

The awful savage goldfish
Sank down to the mud below!
This was at last his journey's end,
With nowhere else to go!

So beware the savage goldfish
With teeth like nine-inch nails!
A mighty chain-saw down his back
And razor-blades for scales!

Beware the savage goldfish!
Beware his evil eye!
But so beware much more, my friends,
The thing that made him die!

21st Century Lullaby

Josephine Gent

Hush, my baby, don't you cry,
No harm will come, I am nearby.
For you I bought this antique bone,
An ivory ring, your very own.
An Elephant gave this for you
To help your baby teeth come through.
I know her baby, left behind,
Was orphaned, but she would not mind,
Another beast would rear her child,
For there were plenty in the wild.

Hush my baby, do not fear,
You are quite safe, your mother's here.
Your furry toys surround your cot,
Panda, Tiger, Ocelot,
Koala Bear and Kangaroo,
Just like the ones kept in the Zoo.
We needed space for you to grow,
And so their forests had to go.
Panda's bamboo made your bed,
Sweet dreams, my little sleepy head.

The dolphin's home is not a pool in a zoo...

Georgina A. Blake

treasured possession...clasped in my hand
I show to a few
who gasp in surprise
that something so transient...is loved

I unfold my palm...
Nothing is there
You accuse me of...madness and lies

You reach for the phone...'How can I treasure air?'
The doctor decided...there was no cure
'For how can you treasure...air?'

You cried...when the ambulance came
Where was my protest...inside?
No time for placard...survey or speech
Could you not see...something one
Cannot possess...is dearest to me?

Shaking your head
You muffle the sound...of my captive voice
as I sing
as I weep
as I sing
as I weep
'Rescue me'
Is a knife wound in the mind
bloodying the soul

Locked away...with book and pen
I read of your blindness

The caged bird...is not happy you know

It longs to fly
The dolphin's home...is not a pool
in a zoo...but the ocean

I write of freedom...in dreams.

Song For The Rare Freshwater Mussel

Di Williams

And here's to you,
To you, Anodonta,
Keep yourself hidden
In the weedy backwaters
Of this industrial England.
Let no lads un-anchor you
From your stony bank
Nor oily dredgers scrape you
From your private waterway.
I wish quiet and peace
To you and yours —
The still marshes
Where the herons hunt
And leech and pondsnail
Crawl about the reeds.
May there always be
Watery hidden reaches
Where you can maintain
Your sanctuary.

Bees and Birds

Gill Blease

Propelled bee,
swoops model plane-like
over me and away,
settling in shaking trees like a bird.
A black speck,
Unbelievably seen.
Baffled bees play their muted trumpets.
This crochet of flowers
The tightened roses their killjoy,
And mine.

Swelling peals,
Suspended fluty warbles
Without origin.
A hidden orator.
Swimming swallows.
These black boomerangs
plunge and float
Like some silent air display.
Ignorance and envy make me
Twice green.

The Dancer

Marguerite Gazeley

I watched her dance,
not leaping high
but moving rhythmically
always connected
to the earth

each step
was praise
thanksgiving,

and as she danced
I understood
why star seekers,
walkers on the moon
had never given me delight.

Only the fear I might feel
for a child, running headlong
before he has a steady footing
on the earth.

Nuclear Fear

Cath Staincliffe

Late summers night.
Through the open window
I hear explosions,
Cracks and muffled thuds.
I check the sound
Against a list of possibles;
Aeroplanes, car crash, doors in the wind,
Someone beating a rug. In the dark?!
Build walls around the thought, buried deep, deep,
  down
(For otherwise it will make me mad)
Of bombs and radiation.
I cannot place the sound.
Walls crumble, my imagination tumbles over

panic ridden decisions, go or stay, how to survive

scene from an old movie
he hands the woman two pills, for herself and the
  child,
she tries to ask whether she should crush it for the
  child,
his grief erupts
the horror of involuntary suicide

rural ganglands
the dispossessed try to steal food
from the farm commandeered by the bully boys
women — the new brood mares

my role
eyes dissolving
glimpse of my son's small face
the skin peeling back

memory
a host of yellow flames abob white paper flowers
chant Hiroshima

The explosions persist
I light on a possible cause,
Search the midnight skies
No visual clues to back me up,
Fireworks.
My stomach begins to unclench
I can bury my fear.
No sirens.
Bury my fear.
Can't ever bury it deep enough.

Mundivagant

Philip Smith

I want to see volcanoes
Baby blind fish in rock pools
Electric storms over forests
I want to see where the lightening struck

I want to see roses growing through the wrecked car
Dance with ghosts in empty houses
I want to see the hands that made the world
Touch the hands that failed it

Ghosts

Pat Amick

Small wonder later Britons colonised
so ruthlessly — the victims of abuse
in turn became abusers — Romanised
and dogmatised as efforts to reduce
the majesty of primal gods of place
cut out the poet's tongue, put closures on
the bridge to Otherworlds, taught songs in praise
of Empire over Anu, Danu, Don.
Uprooted natives soon forget and lay
their parking lots in sacred spaces, handcuff
pilgrims gathered at Stonehenge to pray
— as ancient ghosts abiding long enough
for vindication witness nothing odd
in little forays of The Riot Squad.

A Certain Grief

Georgina A. Blake

to go undaunted
among forest beasts
holds for me
an unexplained fear
handed down for generations
as history
touches those who see
workhouse girls
chimney boys
leaving tears
which time cannot erase

to see a wild beast slaughtered
a dying bird; a fallen tree
a trampled flower
brings to mind
a certain grief
which like the fear
cannot be explained.

Paradigm Shift

This letter is written
To anyone who wishes to listen.

Manchester,
Summer 1989.

Dear Ear,

Lyn Margoulis, a Latin American biologist, has spent much of her life at odds with the biological establishment. However, in co-operation with colleagues, she eventually proved, beyond all reasonable doubt, that human cells came into being by the symbiotic interaction (or co-operation) of at least three previously individual organisms. She is currently a supporter of James Lovelock's Gaia hypothesis which suggests that all the biota of planet Earth have an essential role in maintaining their common environment. Gaia is the Greek goddess of nature.

The poem below is a celebration of her achievements and an affirmation of faith in the living. We are, according to one passage in the bible, supposed to be the GUARDIANS of the Earth, not its abusers.

For twenty years Margoulis toiled at established cell walls,
Selfish genes recoiled, repeating repetitive word;
It's such a complex and competitive world.

From observations intuitive, succinct, seemingly absurd
She found symbiosis in evolution an essential tool
For creation of the mammal, the intelligent and cruel.

Co-operating individuals, so it would appear by this rule,
Are likely to succeed, together, by mutual enhancement;
That steady, unhurried progress of evolutionary refinement.
Now Margoulis and Lovelock sing hymns to Her great government,

Gaia goddess of the good Earth, female principle of life,
Sustaining our collective dream, redeemed, aroused and
alive.

So many years Glory has toiled to be finished beyond
strife,
Queen of Queens recalled, defeating competitive word;
In such a complex, now contemplative world.

I am looking forward, in naive anticipation, to a global future, even as yet barely conceived, its realisation dependent upon co-operation in accord with a new and spirited understanding of evolution.

Thankyou kindly for your attention.

Yours faithfully,
Pete Wilson.

Meat Town

Philip Smith

The sawmill
In the meat town
By the orange waters
And the fairground
By the witches fingers
in the churchyard's end
The children dance
As the moon descends
And the waltzer swings
Whilst the exhaust stings
And the lantern girl sips
At her Singapore Sling
And lays her eyes
And smooths her thighs
And talks to the boys
Who've everything

And the shadow trees swing
Their withered arms
In a strange dance
In the meat town

The big wheel winds
As the sawmill grinds
And the sawdust lays
A feathered sheet
Over the banks
Of the orange river
Where children dip their toes
And curse
And tell how fish once lived
Down there
By the crowfoot banks
And the ethylene tanks
By the ruined arch

In the meat town
In the month of March

And the moon looks down on the meat town

Sonnet for 2002

Pat Amick

Every Age improves upon the last
but never — till the dawning of the new
millenium — were advances made so fast;
had mother lived to see Two-Thousand-Two
her faith in men of learning would be quite
restored; the surge in cancers is confined,
productive life is possible in spite
of it — we seldom risk the unrefined
parched air outside the workhouse anymore.
She got contaminated things to eat
but here The Board supports the active poor
with all the food the labs can simulate
and purple skin and baldness brings no shame —
she'd feel so pretty now we're all the same.

I've Gone Green

P. D. Cookson

Hey I've dumped all
Those old aerosols
And bought the CFC free
I've gone green
Just like Mrs T

Hey I've dumped
Those packet dinners
And bought additives free
I've gone green
Just like Mrs T

Hey I'll give up smoking
I'm not joking
A new healthy fit and active me
I've gone green
Just like Mrs T

Hey Maybe I'll dump the poor
And close some schools
And start a war
And imprison leftist fools
And raise interest rates
And refuse to advocate the use of mates
And live in a house
Down south with big iron gates
And keep the unemployed at bay
And never say the word gay
And teargas demonstrators
Or wash them all away
Hey Maybe I will go green
And then I'll turn mean
And try to get elected VIP MP
Just like Mrs T

Litterbug Lovers

Lorna Euphemia Griffiths

The next time that you get the urge
to find a field or grassy verge
in which to romp and roll and lust
A warning, if condoms are a must
Beware the dangers of impulsive oats
Not just for you but for grazing goats
For discarding condoms at your leisure
can cause the cows and bulls displeasure
or even death
and that's no joke
'Coz chomping rubber they will choke
So to avoid the issue of litter too
Bring a bag and take them home with you!

Feeding Birds

Jean Tarry

Morning.
Blackbird
Scatters his song
Like diamonds
In a silky blue sky.
Daisies
With silver rays,
Golden hearts
Mimic the sun.
Brocaded bees
Gather to drink
The elderflower wine.
I
Rush outside
With crumbs, nuts, fruit, scraps.
Unthinkingly
Meddling with perfection.

Dear Tree

Julia Damassa

Was it worth your life
for my words?
What part of you
is the pencil I hold?
Can you feel
marks on the paper?
Is it right
that you should suffer
so we may write
about suffering?
Tell me what you want to say.

A Don't Know Vote For Green

Michael Nolan

They dug up the weeds,
Planted rhododendrons
And voted green.

Biographies

Mark Abraham

I teach maths in Salford, and have lived in Manchester for fifteen years. My efforts at verse combine an interest in music and writing. I often get ideas from my son Luke, aged eight.

Pat Amick

After teaching, I relax with the children in our garden beside the (rather dirty) River Irwell in Rossendale. Here that combination of motorway noise, papermill stink and awesome natural beauty inspires me to write.

Julie Armstrong-Colton

I am 31 years old and have lived in the North West most of my life apart from a short stint spent in Amsterdam and Brussels. I have a daughter Yasmin who is three and I currently teach English part-time at South Cheshire College.

Georgina A. Blake

I wrote my first poem when I was eight years old and I've been interested in writing ever since. My inspiration has been life, people, and the love of words which I hope I will never lose.

Gill Blease

I am nineteen years old, and have just completed an art foundation course, prior to starting a Fine Art degree at Newcastle University. My main interests are painting and drawing — though being published in *No Earthly Reason?* has certainly encouraged me to write more.

Debjani Chatterjee

My books include: *I Was That Woman* (Hippopotamus), *The Elephant-Headed God and Other Hindu Tales* (Lutterworth) and *The Role of Religion in 'A Passage To India'* (Writers Workshop, Calcutta). I am Sheffield's Principal Community Relations Officer.

Gwyneth Cleworth
I was an evacuee from London to Bedfordshire, and then my birthplace, Bolton. Having raised a family, I returned to study and poetry. My work draws upon my experience in life and interest in people, travel and world affairs.

P. D. Cookson
I was born in 1965 in Manchester and started writing in 1985 when I joined Commonword via the Northern Gay Writers. I have appeared in two previous publications: *Poetic Licence* published in 1987 and 'Get Out More', a cassette made by Northern Gay Writers in 1987. My interests are acting, snooker, reading, performing and slagging off the Tories at every opportunity.

Tim Court
I am a student who has recently moved to the Wigan area. As well as a passionate affection for the natural world, I enjoy reading, writing, art and music.

Julia Damassa
I am a 23 year old drama teacher working at a comprehensive school in Wigan, but living in the Manchester area where I am involved in various community theatre projects. I studied at Bangor University and have a love of Welsh literature.

Marguerite Gazeley
A bookworm — devouring books with such relish, I feel a threat to forests! From my mother, a love of writing; she, at a loss without a pen, and I, more often, at a loss for words...

Josephine Gent
I am a mother of three, grandmother of four and live in a house that belongs to three cats. A member of Marple writers' workshop, this is my first appearance in print.

Lorna Euphemia Griffiths
I am 24 years old, born and bred in Bolton, Lancashire of Jamaican parents. I now live in Manchester. I started to write when I was eighteen years old. I am now published in 'Art Attack', *Talkers Through Dream Doors* and 'Blackboard'.

Michael Hall
I am a 31 year old teacher working at Leacroft School in Manchester. I have a wife and three children. Interests include: rock-climbing, canoeing, mountain leading, theatre, music. I have been writing for four years.

K. M. McDonnell
31 years old, married with two young daughters, I recently left full-time employment to attempt a career in writing. I am involved in a community sports project and enjoy reading, writing and political satire. This will be my first published work.

Jane McNulty
Aged 34 years, I was born in the one-time 'steel town' outside Manchester, where I still live with my family — includes a daughter and three dogs! I am a Green Party member.

Maria Maryon
I grew up in Stevenage, and came to Manchester in 1987. Since coming here I have been involved in two writing groups and this has given me plenty of ideas for my writing as well as lots of encouragement to keep going.

Jerry Middleton
I moved to Manchester eighteen months ago. My employment record ranges from QE2 to milkman and back. I am a member of Manchester Poets and an excited father to be.

Michael Nolan
I was born in Salford and grew up in Miles Platting. I started writing seriously about six years ago. I share the same birthday as Stevie Wonder.

Diane R. Pickering
I live in Lees, Oldham and am 27 years old. I am a member of the 'Oldham Wordsmiths'. Last year we published a book called *First Edition*. My favourite poets include Sylvia Plath and Dylan Thomas.

Joan Poulson
I was born in Manchester, have three children, and am trained in teaching and in therapeutic massage. I work as a free-lance writer and workshop organiser and believe that writing can be a valuable therapy. In late 1989 I began a project in psychiatric day centres. I support the theory of deep ecology and the work of environmental and anti-apartheid groups.

Margaret Rich
As a mother, a teacher and a Christian I am mindful of the heritage to be passed on to future generations.

Steve Rouse
I'm a 26 year old civil servant, with a passion for contemporary classical music and minimalist art. Other interests include painting, Mensa, and the BBC Philharmonic Club.

Philip Smith
I was conceived, born, raised, educated and now pay rent in a town much like any other. I am aged 25 and trying to write for a living.

Cath Staincliffe
I'm a free-lance cultural worker, I do drama projects with community groups. When I'm not busy with that (or parenting), I love reading — feminist, sci-fi and crime books, and writing. I am a member of Commonword's Women Writers' workshop.

Peggy Stockwell
After my husband died I started writing. This developed when I joined a writers' group. Other interests include: swimming, gardening, listening to music, walking and holidays abroad. I have two daughters and a grandson.

Jean Tarry
Ex-scouser, ex-local government officer, now part-time voluntary worker at the Psychological Medicine Unit, Christie Hospital, I edit the quarterly magazine 'Never Bury Poetry'. My hobbies are: running, reading, writing, rambling, 'rithmetic...

Elaine Tebay
Born Manchester, moved to Stockport late fifties with my husband. Hill walking, flora and fauna are my loves. Each month I meet two writers (and friends) survivors of a creative writing class (1986).

Steven Waling
I've been published in various magazines and anthologies, including *Between Mondays* and *Poetic Licence*, and in a booklet 'Riding Shotgun' which came out earlier this year. I'm unemployed, but only according to the Government.

Di Williams
I started writing poems while studying biology at school, and continue to draw on images from nature in songs, stories and other pieces since. I am a folk singer, and a comic performer at rallies in support of ecological and other issues.

Pete Wilson
Soon my life will begin (at forty). I have just graduated; BSc (Hons) Environmental Sciences. I seek ecologically sound and socially useful employment. The job centre said I would be treated as an adult now.

About Commonword

Commonword is a non-profitmaking community publishing co-operative, producing books by writers in the North West, and supporting and developing their work. In this way Commonword brings new writing to a wide audience.

Over a period of ten years Commonword has published poetry, short stories and other forms of creative writing. *No Earthly Reason?* is the sixth title to be published under the **Crocus** imprint. Forthcoming books include *Relative To Me...*, a collection of short stories about families.

In general, Commonword seeks to encourage the creative writing and publishing of the diverse groups in society who have lacked, or been excluded from, the means of expression through the written word. Working class writers, black writers, women, and lesbians and gay men all too often fall into this category.

To give writers the opportunity to develop their work in an informal setting, Commonword offers a variety of writers' workshops, such as Womanswrite, the Monday Night Group, and Northern Gay Writers.

Cultureword which is a part of Commonword, and which acts as a focus for Asian and Afro-Caribbean writers, organises the Identity Writers' Workshop. Cultureword also co-ordinates 'Identity' magazine, and a writing competition for Black writers.

In addition to writers' workshops and publishing, Commonword offers a manuscript reading service to give constructive criticism, and can give information and advice to writers about facilities in their immediate locality. 'Writers Reign' magazine contains both information and new writing.

Commonword is supported by: the Association of Greater Manchester Authorities, North West Arts and Manchester Education Committee.

The Commonword/Cultureword offices are at Cheetwood House, 21 Newton Street, Piccadilly, Manchester. Our phone number is (061) 236 2773. We would like to hear from you.

If you've enjoyed reading No Earthly Reason?, *why not try some of our other recent books?*

Talkers Through Dream Doors
Fourteen talented Black women write about their lives in *Talkers Through Dream Doors*, a collection of poetry and short stories. Through anger, laughter, and gentle reflection, they show us the world as they see it. Each expresses their identity in a distinctive and memorable style — from the cosmopolitan observations of Cindy Artiste to Jolina Black's down to earth humour in 'Ebony Baby Girl'. This collection is often moving, sometimes shocking, and it constantly presents an affirmation of the strength and creativity of Black women writers today.
"The full potential of Black women writers has not yet been realised. A book like **Talkers Through Dream Doors** *can only aid the process, and with such high standards, these women are going to spearhead the campaign." (Caribbean Times)*
£3.50 120 pages ISBN 0 946745 60 9

Now Then
This new collection of poetry and short stories looks at lifestyles, work and leisure from 1945 to the present day. In 'Home For Whitsun' Elsie Maskell recalls the spectacle and excitement of the Salford Whit Walks. Ron Redshaw relives his comical boyhood adventures down by the river in 'Going Back On The Irwell'. Change and continuity is looked at humorously by Maureen Tottoh in 'For Judy', as she compares the fashions of then and now. For other writers it is their experiences of the world of work that remain the most vivid, as Nell Harwood depicts in 'It's My Life Isn't It?' These are just a small selection from the writing contained in *Now Then* which powerfully evokes the flavour of a crucial period in recent history.
"This book gives a vivid account of a host of changes ... sometimes funny, sometimes cynical, the authors give a down-to-earth view of Northern working-class life." (Oldham Evening Chronicle)
£3.50 108 pages ISBN 0 946745 55 2

She Says

She Says is a new collection from five women writers celebrating the vitality and variety of women's poetry today. Pat Amick writes movingly and skilfully about her feelings for her father, of childhood joys and of the bitter-sweet nature of romance. Cathy Bolton's work deals with relationships, and the way in which they are constantly cut across by questions of power, the past and sexuality. Anne Paley's poetry has a searching and reflective quality, whilst describing situations that affect many women. Sheila Parry uses powerful images, culled from folklore, myths and fairytales, in her work, whilst Cath Staincliffe expresses her thoughts about love, motherhood and politics in a way that is always challenging and original.

"This collection of poems is rich and varied in form and content and always thought provoking. Read it." (7 DAYS)

£2.95 96 pages ISBN 0 946745 50 1

Black and Priceless

Black and Priceless is an exciting collection of poetry and short stories by Black writers. The skill of Asian women's writing is illustrated by the work of Deepa Banerjee and Debjani Chatterjee, whilst in Peter Kalu's 'The Adventures of Maud Mellington', we have a hilarious detective story with a difference. The poetry of John Lyons tells with passion and energy of the experience of living with racism in this country, whilst Sally Neaser writes movingly of her feelings about motherhood. This selection of twenty-one writers includes those who are fast becoming familiar names, alongside others for whom this book represents their debut in print. A highly readable and diverse collection, *Black and Priceless* reflects the power of Black ink!

*"All the pieces in this work have a positive strength, and the direct use of language is raw and powerful...***Black and Priceless** *is a timely eruption of a new and expressive black consciousness." (CITY LIFE)*

£3.50 200 pages ISBN 0 946745 45 5

Holding Out: Short Stories by Women

Holding Out contains a compelling and challenging selection of writing. With both humour and pathos, this collection vividly portrays women's lives. The stories in the book take the reader from a still birth in 1930's Lancashire in 'The Confinement', through to a disturbing tale of child sex abuse in 1980's Britain in 'Daddy's Toy'. 'A Pair of Jeans' describes how what may appear to be a simple item of clothing can wreak havoc in the life of an Asian family, whilst 'Nothing Happened' is an affectionately wry look at life

on the dole. These are just a small selection from this collection of twenty-one stories, which demonstrates both the strength, and the variety, of contemporary women's writing.
"This impressive collection of new work is sincere and honest, and it's enjoyable because the women featured cope with their lives with strength, courage and most of all, humour." (CITY LIFE)
£3.50 156 pages ISBN 0 946745 30 7

Autobiography

Australian Journal: Alf Ironmonger 60p
In 1946, off the coast of South Australia, two young shipmates decide to jump ashore. This is their tale...
ISBN 0 946745 01 3 64 pages

Dobroyed: Leslie Wilson £1.20
The unique inside story of one person's experience of a year spent in an approved school.
ISBN 0 950599 74 3 142 pages

Fiction

Marshall's Big Score: John Gowling £1.20
A book about a love affair, played out against the backdrop of the gay scene in London, Liverpool and Manchester.
ISBN 0 946745 03 X 76 pages

Turning Points: Northern Gay Writers £2.95
This collection of short stories and poetry explores moments of crisis - turning points - in the lives of a variety of characters, with various different conclusions...
ISBN 0 946745 20 X 120 pages

Poetry

Poetic Licence £2.50
Poetic Licence is an exuberant and bubbling brew of poetry from a diversity of poets living and working in Greater Manchester. Their work celebrates the many pleasures of poetry from the serious and intense, to the playful and humorous.
ISBN 0 946745 40 4 208 pages

Between Mondays: The Monday Night Group £2.50
This collection of poetry is the latest book from Commonword's Monday Night Group. It brings together some promising new writers with plenty to say about life in the city, sexuality, Catholicism and many other subjects.
ISBN 0 946745 35 8 104 pages

Liberation Soldier: Joe Smythe £2.50
Employing a variety of styles, Joe explores the discontents and disturbances of the times, from inner city riots to apartheid in South Africa.
ISBN 0 946745 25 0 84 pages

Hermit Crab: Di Williams 30p
Using the imagery of the sea and the seashore, these poems tell of a daughter's journey towards independence.
ISBN 0 946745 15 3 28 pages

Consider Only This: Sarah Ward 30p
A selection of poems which captures the atmosphere of moorland, cotton mills and small town life.
ISBN 0 946745 04 8 28 pages

Diary of A Divorce: Wendy Whitfield £1.00
Wendy Whitfield reflects on the breakdown of her marriage in a series of poems and cartoons.
ISBN 0 9505997 7 8 28 pages

Forthcoming Titles

Relative to me... £3.95
Families — love 'em or hate 'em, this book of short stories will both move and delight you.
ISBN 0 946745 70 6 Publication date: 14 February 1990

Order Form

TITLE	QUANTITY	PRICE	AMOUNT
Talkers Through Dream Doors		£3.50	
Now Then		£3.50	
She Says		£2.95	
Black and Priceless		£3.50	
Holding Out		£3.50	
Poetic Licence		£2.50	
Between Mondays		£2.50	
Liberation Soldier		£2.50	
Turning Points		£2.95	
Hermit Crab		30p	
Consider Only This		30p	
Marshall's Big Score		£1.20	
Dobroyed		£1.20	
Australian Journal		60p	
Diary of A Divorce		£1.00	
Relative to me...		£3.95	
		TOTAL	

Please send a cheque or postal order, made payable to Commonword Ltd, covering the purchase price plus 25p per book postage and packing.

NAME: ....

ADDRESS: ....

....

.... Postcode ....

Please return to: Commonword, Cheetwood House, 21 Newton Street, Manchester M1 1FZ.